PEOPLE WHO HELP US

Nurse

Alison Cooper and Diana Bentley

Photographs by
Chris Fairclough

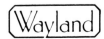

People Who Help Us

Ambulance Crew
Bus Driver
Firefighter
Flight Attendant
Lifeboat Crew
Nurse
Police Officer
Train Driver
Vet

Designer: David Armitage

First published in 1990 by
Wayland (Publishers) Ltd
61 Western Road, Hove
East Sussex, BN3 1JD, England

British Library Cataloguing in Publication Data
Cooper, Alison
  Nurse
  1. Great Britain. Medicine. Nursing
  I. Title II. Series
  610.73'0941

  ISBN 1–85210–849–5

Typeset by Rachel Gibbs, Wayland
Printed and bound in Belgium by Casterman S.A.

Contents

Words that are <u>underlined</u> appear
in the glossary on page 30.

Tony is a charge nurse.

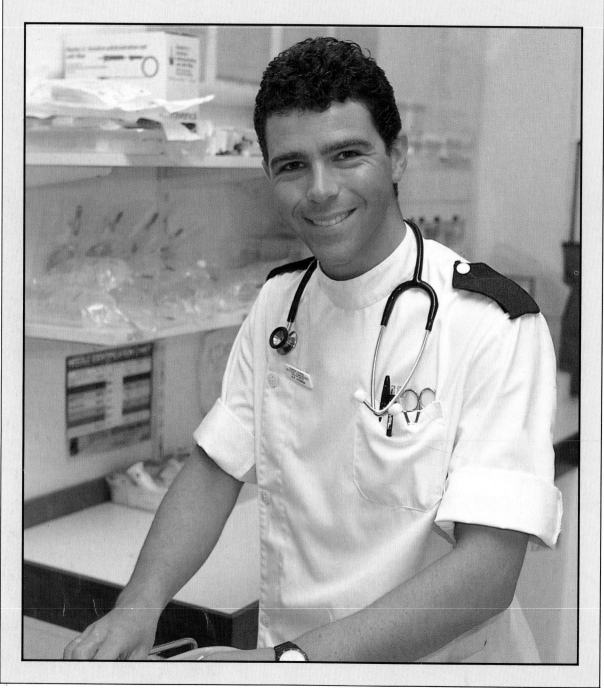

Charge nurses are the head nurses in their departments. Tony works in the accident department of a big hospital.

Tony is just starting work. He is taking over now from Kate. She tells him all about the accidents that she has had to deal with.

Alex has had an accident.

Alex is on holiday from school. She has been riding her bike. But look! She has crashed into some railings and fallen off.

Anna rings for an ambulance.

Anna is Alex's mum. She calls the doctor and tells him about Alex's accident. He tells her to take Alex to the hospital. Anna rings for an ambulance.

Alex goes to hospital in the ambulance.

The ambulance crew are taking Alex to the accident department. They have put a <u>sling</u> on her arm to stop it from moving about too much.

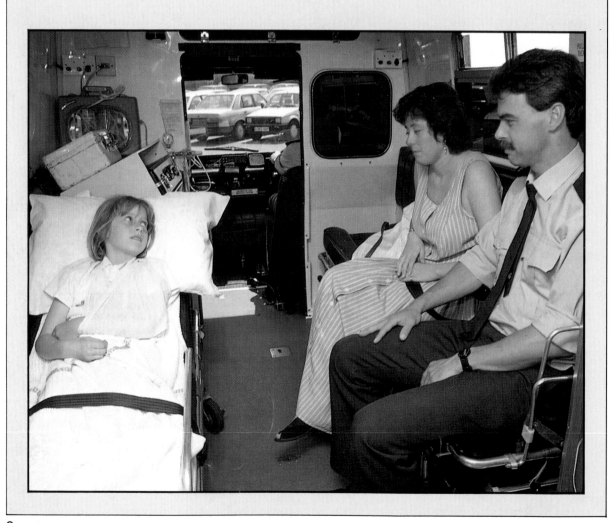

Hospitals have special entrances for ambulances, so that people who are very sick can be taken into the hospital quickly. The ambulance crew take Alex into the hospital.

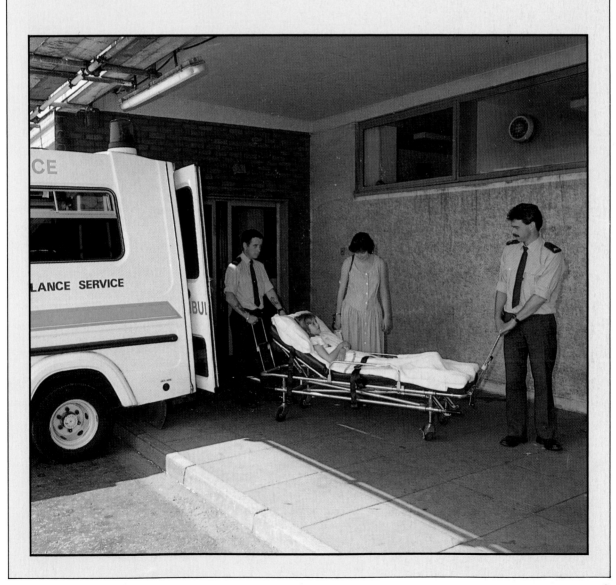

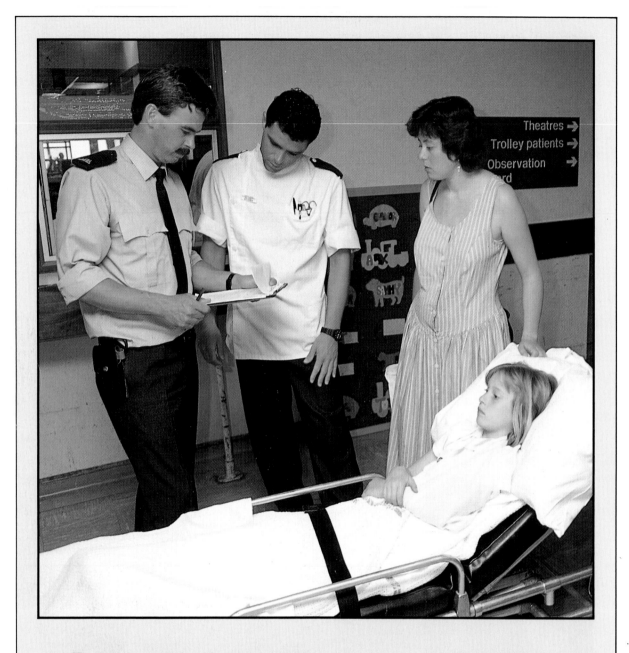

Tony meets them at the entrance. He says
hello to Alex. He looks at her arm and at
the cut on her knee.

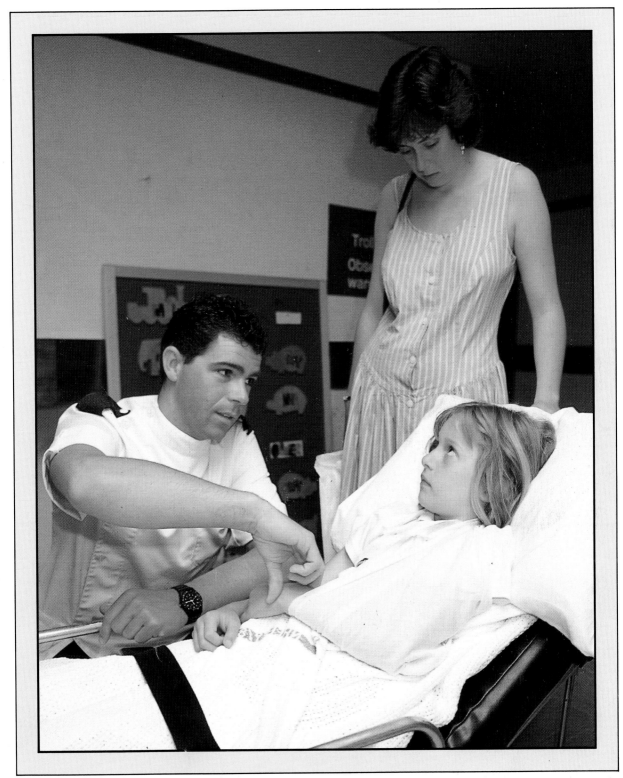

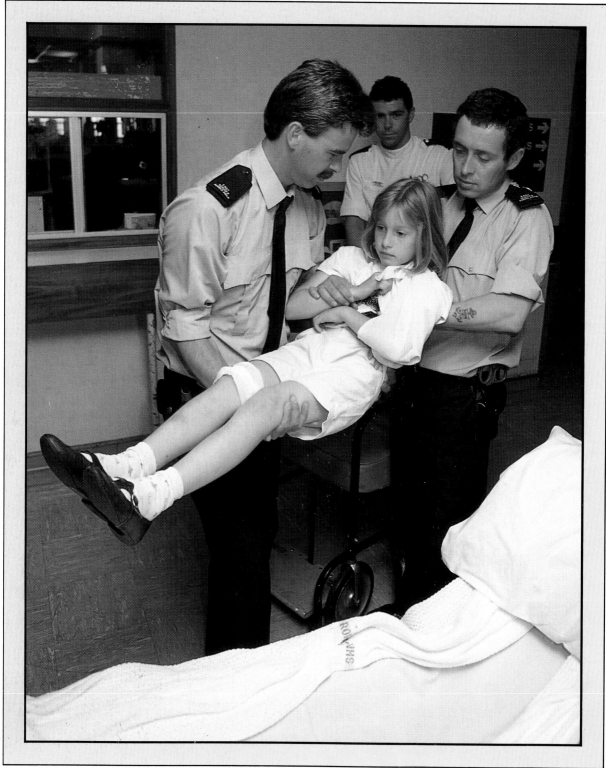

Alex is not feeling very well because her arm hurts. The ambulance crew lift her into a wheelchair, so that she does not have to walk. Then Tony wheels her to the waiting room.

This is the waiting room.

If you have an accident, you usually have to wait here to see the hospital doctors. The doctors and nurses have to treat those people who are badly hurt first, but they will help Alex as soon as they can.

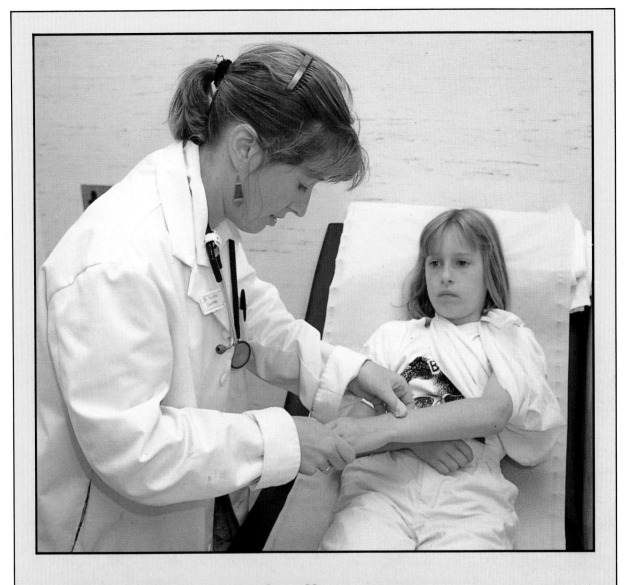

This is the examination room.

The doctor is ready to <u>examine</u> Alex now. Alex's arm may be broken. She needs to have an X-ray.

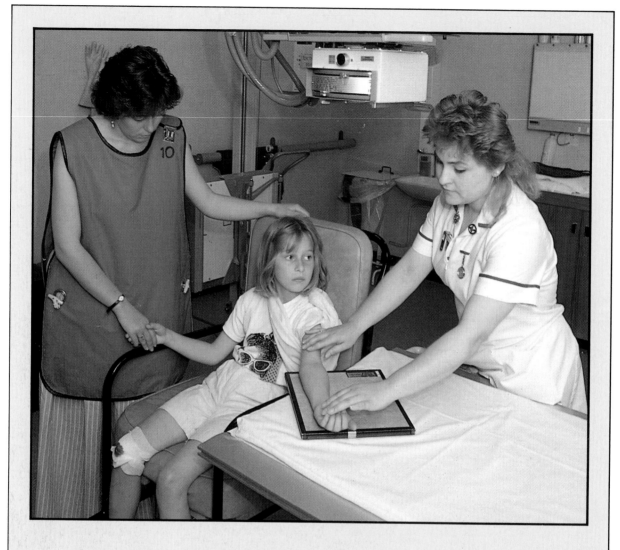

Alex has an X-ray.

In the X-ray room the <u>radiographer</u>
carefully puts Alex's arm in the right place.
The X-ray machine takes a picture of the
bones inside Alex's arm.

Tony makes a <u>plaster cast</u>.

The X-ray picture shows Alex has a broken bone in her wrist. Tony is going to put a plaster cast on her arm. This will help the bone to get better because it will stop it from moving about. First, Tony wraps a soft bandage round Alex's arm.

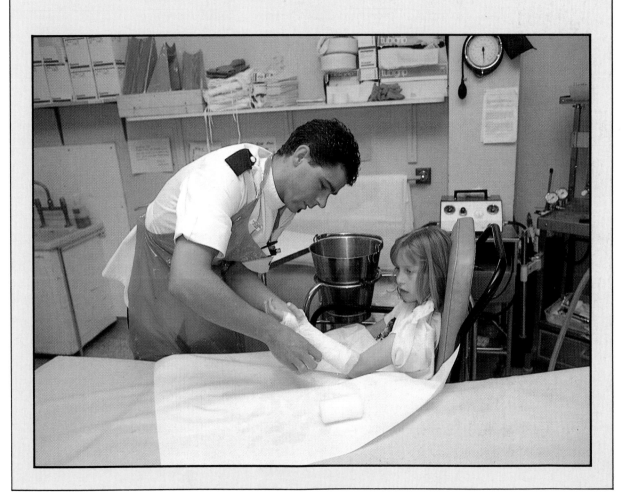

Then he wets some <u>plaster of Paris</u>.

Tony covers the soft bandage with the plaster of Paris. It is very wet and sticky! When it dries, the plaster will be hard and it will protect Alex's arm if she bumps into anything.

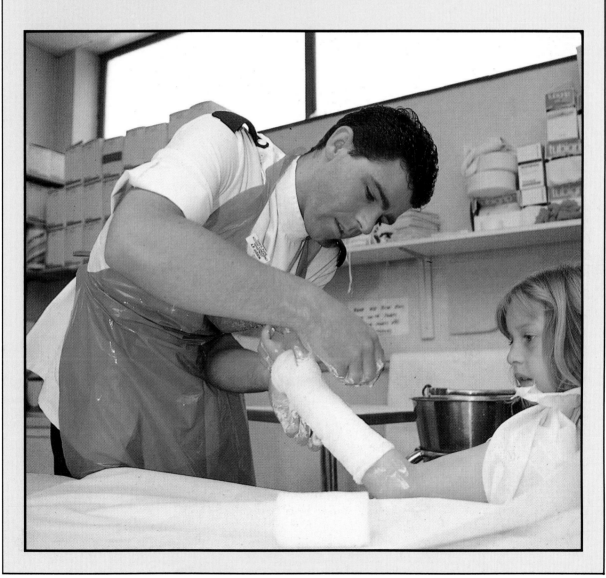

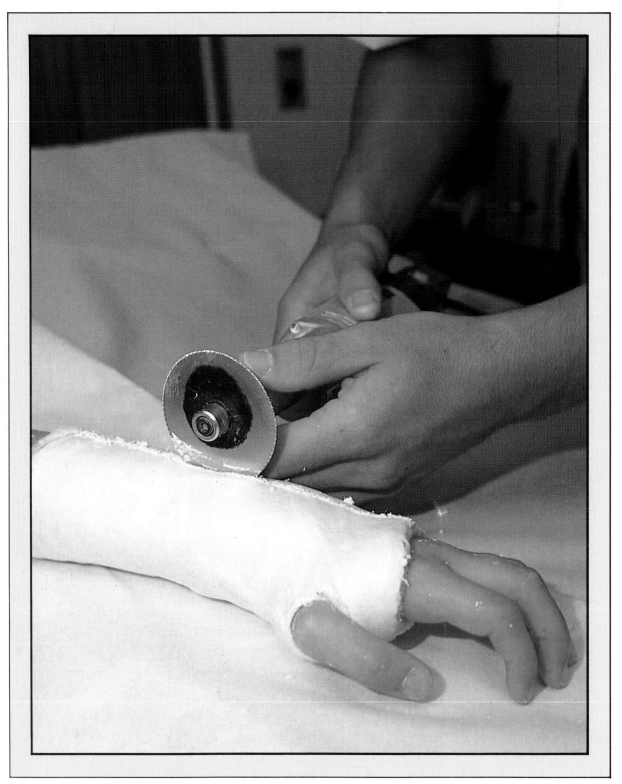

Tony switches on the plaster saw. He tells Alex not to worry – he is only going to split the plaster! If he did not do this, the plaster might become too tight and make her arm sore.

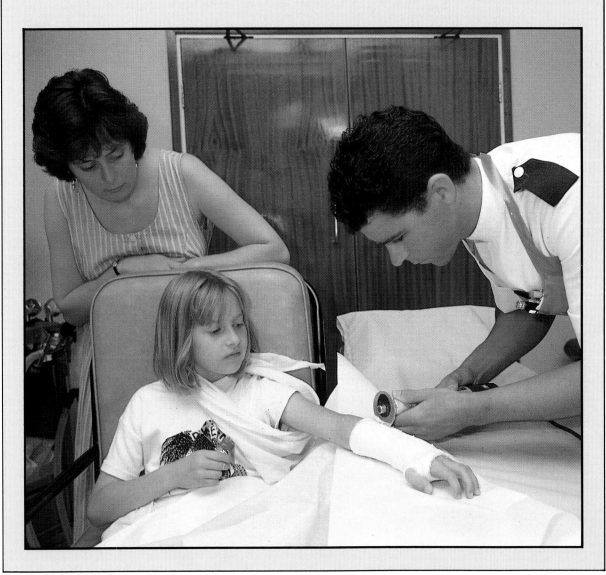

Tony stitches Alex's cut knee.

Tony cleans Alex's knee with some
<u>antiseptic</u>. This is to make sure the cut does
not become <u>infected</u>.

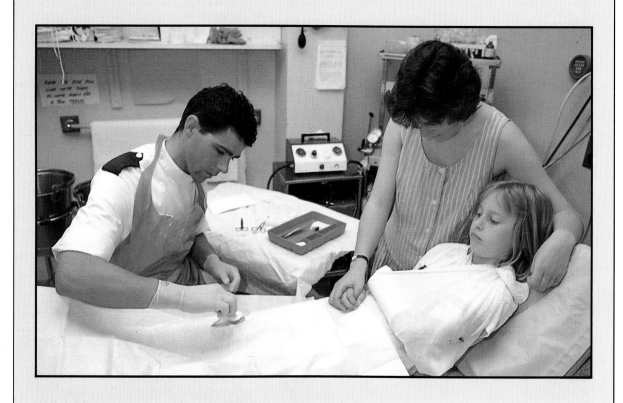

Tony fills a <u>syringe</u> with <u>anaesthetic</u>. He is
going to <u>inject</u> it into Alex's knee. Then it will
not hurt when Tony stitches the cut.

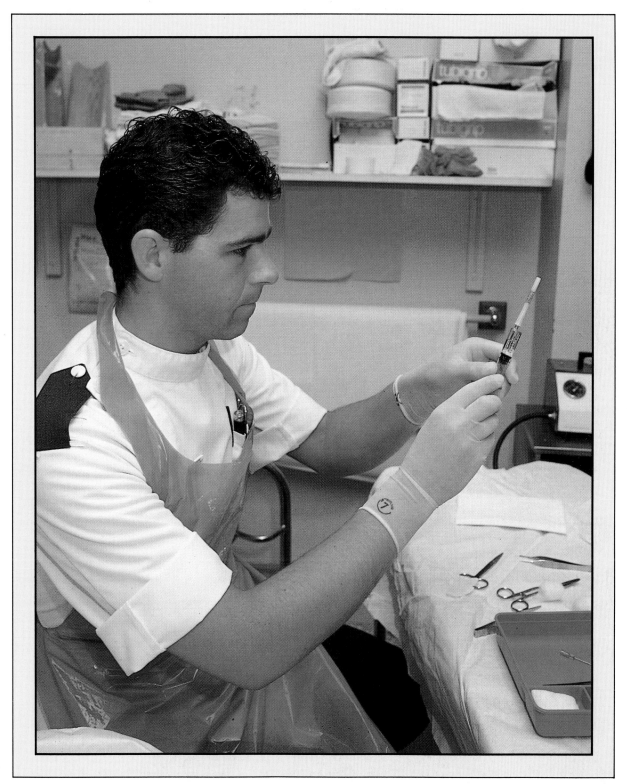

Tony uses a special needle and thread to stitch the cut. The stitches hold the cut together and help it to get better. Alex cannot feel anything – but she does not want to look! She talks to Anna instead.

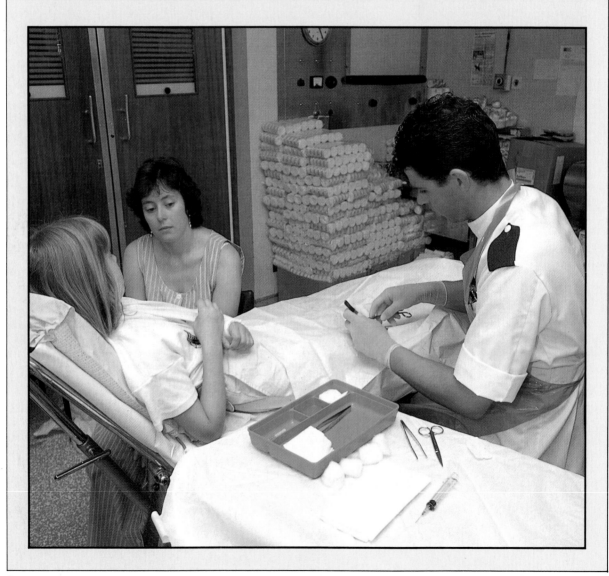

Tony puts a clean <u>dressing</u> on Alex's knee to keep the dirt away from the cut.

Needles and syringes are dangerous and must not be left lying around once they have been used. Tony makes sure that they are thrown into a special bin.

Alex and Anna go home.

Tony tells Anna to bring Alex to the hospital clinic next week so that he can make sure her arm is healing properly. Then he says goodbye to them.

Anna and Alex go to the reception desk.
They make an <u>appointment</u> for the hospital
clinic. At last they can go home. Alex is
starting to feel much better now. Anna says
she has been very brave.

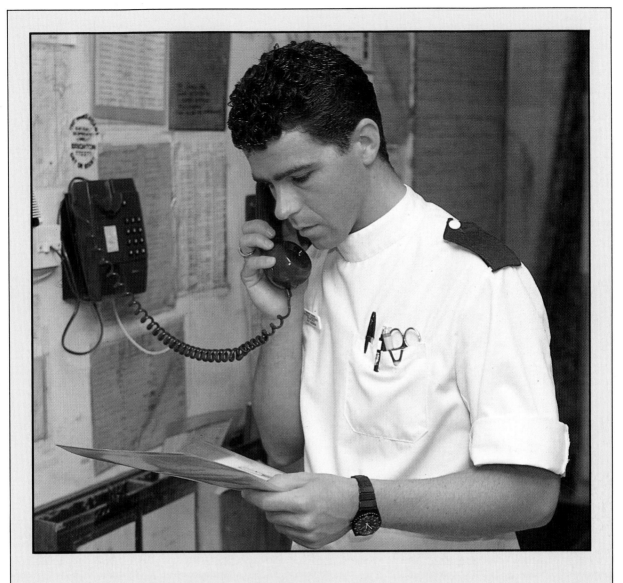

A doctor rings Tony.

There are some more patients for Tony to look after now. The accident department is very busy today.

Glossary

<u>Anaesthetic</u>   A liquid that stops people from feeling pain when they are having an operation.

<u>Antiseptic</u>   A chemical that kills germs.

<u>Appointment</u>   A time when a doctor or nurse arranges to examine a patient.

<u>Clinic</u>   A place where you go to see a doctor or have special treatment in a hospital.

<u>Dressing</u>   A pad of soft material used to cover a cut or graze.

<u>Examine</u>   Look carefully at someone to find out what treatment they need.

<u>Infected</u>   Full of germs.

<u>Inject</u>   Put liquid into someone's body using a needle and syringe.

<u>Plaster cast</u>   A hard case that is used to protect broken bones.

<u>Plaster of Paris</u>   A white powder that can be made into plaster casts while it is wet. When it dries it becomes very hard.

<u>Radiographer</u>   A person who works an X-ray machine.

<u>Sling</u>   A triangular piece of material. It is used to support an arm or wrist.

<u>Syringe</u>   A plastic tube that holds the liquid used for injections.

Books to read

First Aid (series) Dorothy Baldwin and Claire Lister (Wayland, 1986)

Hospital John Colerne (Franklin Watts, 1988)

My Visit to the Hospital Sophie Davies and Diana Bentley (Wayland, 1989)

Nurse (Gujerati/English) Brenda Clarke (Franklin Watts, 1986)

Nurse (Urdu/English) Brenda Clarke (Franklin Watts, 1986)

The Nurse Anne Stewart (Hamish Hamilton, 1984)

Index

Acknowledgements

The authors and publishers would like to thank the following for
their help in the preparation of this book: The Director of Nursing
Services and all staff in the Accident and Emergency
Department, Royal Sussex County Hospital; the Chief Ambulance
Officer and staff, East Sussex Ambulance Service and Alex
Breedon. All incidents shown were specially arranged.